Mel Bay Presents **THE JIMMY BRUNO JAZZ GUITAR SERIES . . .**

Six Essential
FINGERINGS
for the JAZZ
GUITARIST

by

JIMMY BRUNO

Cover Photo by Gina Benedetto
Headstock of BENEDETTO "Jimmy Bruno" model prototype

2 3 4 5 6 7 8 9 0

Visit us on the Web at www.melbay.com — E-mail us at email@melbay.com

Contents

Acknowledgments

Special thanks to the following people who have helped and encouraged me to write such a book.

My Wife Peggy

My Son Jimmy (served as my editor)

Bob & Cindy Benedetto (Benedetto Guitars)

Rich Raezer (Raezer's Edge Cabinets)

Ed Benson (Just Jazz Guitar Magazine)

Marc Dicciani (University of the Arts)

Tommy Gumina (Polytone Amplifiers)

Bill Schultz (Fender Musical Instruments)

Bill Acton (Guild Guitars)

Ritchie Fliegler

"The breadth and depth of Jimmy Bruno's knowledge of jazz guitar is astounding. In this text, his lofty methodology is brought down to earth. As in his performances, the very soul of Jimmy's wisdom is laid bare, with a generosity and unique straightforwardness all his own. How appropriate that someone affectionately nicknamed Paganini should, like the revolutionary violinist, equally impart such enlightenment!"
CINDY BENEDETTO

"Jimmy Bruno's harmonic melodic concept along with his astounding technique is enough to make any guitarist (in any style) turn green with envy. If this book can shed a little light on how he reached this stature I definitely want a copy!!"
CHARLES H. CHAPMAN, PROFESSOR, BERKLEE COLLEGE OF MUSIC

If you have any questions feel free to e-mail me at jimmy@jimmybruno.com

Introduction

main obstacle facing every guitarist is the overwhelming number of fingering possibilities. After thirty some
of playing professionally I have found these six fingerings for the major scales to be the most efficient. From
six fingerings all other scales are derived. As guitarists we face too many choices as to where to play a given
note or phrase. It is this phenomenon of the instrument that hinders one's ability to make sound and hand associations.
In other words, "What sound will I get if I put my 1st finger down on the 3rd string, 5th fret, and how does it relate
to the note that comes before it or after it; how does it sound against a given chord?

A saxophone player does not have this problem. The fingerings are fixed. After years of using fingering x, y,
z, he is used to hearing the same sound. After years of this repetitive process the average saxophone player develops
a fairly decent ear and a remarkable technique. It is this limitless choice facing the guitarist that hinders his
development as a musician. The purpose of this book is to eliminate all unnecessary fingerings. Just because it is
possible to play a given scale or phrase with fingering "A", "B", or "C" does not make it practical.

I have compiled what I believe to be a standard set of fingerings for the instrument. Furthermore, the fingerings
are as symmetrical as possible. For instance, the various degrees of the scale are kept on the same finger throughout
each pair of fingerings.

The guitar is a very visual instrument. I believe it is imperative to visualize each fingering until it can be mentally
practiced without your instrument. After a few months, you should be able to associate the sounds with the mental
pictures. A pianist, for example, can see each scale and all of its notes. The picture never changes for him; it is
repeated approximately 7 times. Below each scale I have included what I call a "mental picture". This is what I see
when I look at the fingerboard if improvising from a major scale. It is not a chord grid. It is the fingerboard laid out
horizontally in the following manner:

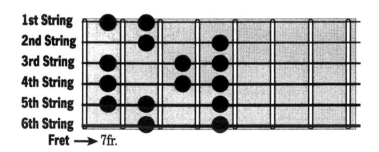

I have named the six fingerings as follows:

- The 1st pair – **6V2, 5V2**
- The 2nd pair – **6V4, 5V4**
- The 3rd pair – **6H2, 5H2**

Translation:

- **6** = starts on the 6th string
- **V** = crosses the neck in a vertical direction
- **2** = starts with the 2nd finger
- **H** = crosses the neck horizontally

For example: 5H2 means the fingering starts on the 5th string, crosses the neck horizontally and starts with the
2nd finger. The horizontal pairs are perfectly symmetrical while the other pairs are symmetrical except for the last
few notes. Once the six basic fingerings are mastered all this becomes quite obvious. I cannot stress enough the
importance of thoroughly mastering the six basic fingerings before proceeding to the other fingerings. A complete
mental picture is necessary before you try to connect the mental pictures. I have purposely illustrated only two
examples (see page 11). To fully grasp this concept it is necessary for you to explore this aspect on your own. Spelling
it out defeats the purpose. The same is true if you skip ahead to the other fingerings. If you find yourself not
understanding where the scales are derived from, STOP! Go back… you need more practice.

Jimmy Bruno

The Major Scales
Vertical Fingerings
2nd Finger

6 = starting string

V = vertical

2 = starting finger

6V2

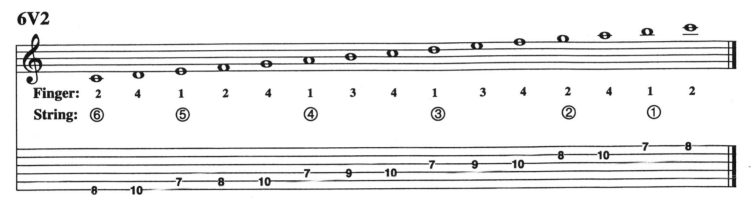

Finger:	2	4	1	2	4	1	3	4	1	3	4	2	4	1	2
String:	⑥		⑤			④			③			②		①	

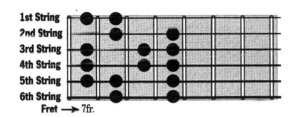

Mental Picture

It is imperative that you visualize the scale

5V2

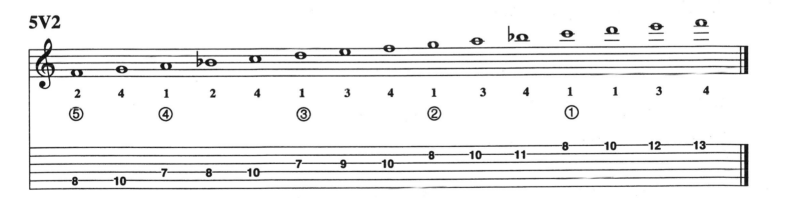

2	4	1	2	4	1	3	4	1	3	4	1	1	3	4
⑤		④			③			②			①			

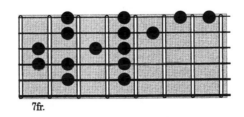

Practice Tip

mportant to practice these fingerings in all twelve keys. Below is the recommended procedure.

Key	Fingering	Starting Fret
C	6V2	8
F	5V2	8
B♭	6V2	6
E♭	5V2	6
A♭	6V2	4
D♭	5V2	4
G♭	6V2	2
B	5V2	2
E	5V2	7
A	6V2	5
D	5V2	5
G	6V2	3
C	5V2	3

Practice this until all fingerings create a mental picture. Make sure you practice the scales descending as well as ascending.

Try using the fingerings to solo over II - V - I progressions in all keys.

Example: Dm7 - G7 - CMa7 = use fingering **6V2**

Gm7 - C7 - FMa7 = use fingering **5V2**

Cm7 - F7 - B♭Ma7 = use fingering **6V2**, etc.

Vertical Fingerings
4th Finger

6V4

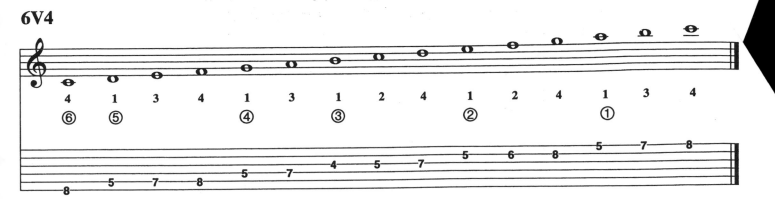

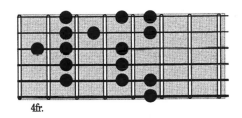

4fr.

5V4

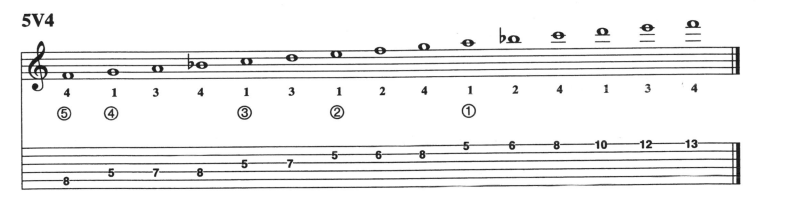

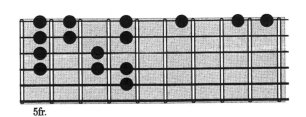

5fr.

Here is the same thing with the 6V4 and 5V4

Key	Fingering	Starting Fret
C	6V4	8
F	5V4	8
B♭	6V4	6
E♭	5V4	6
A♭	6V4	4
D♭	5V4	4
G♭	5V4	9
B	6V4	7
E	5V4	7
A	6V4	5
D	5V4	5
G	5V4	10
C	6V4	8

Solo over II - V - I progressions in all keys.

Example: Dm7 - G7 - CMa7 = use fingering **6V4**

Gm7 - C7 - FMa7 = use fingering **5V4**

Cm7 - F7 - B♭Ma7 = use fingering **6V4**, etc.

Horizontal Fingerings

6H2

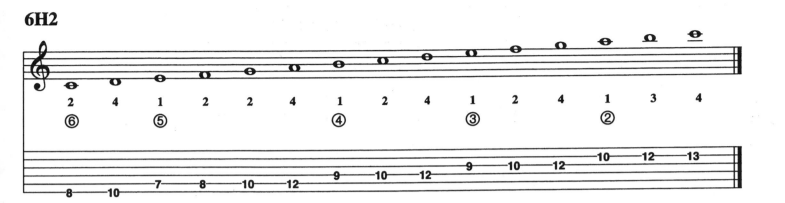

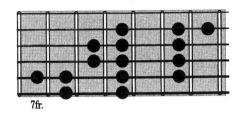

5H2

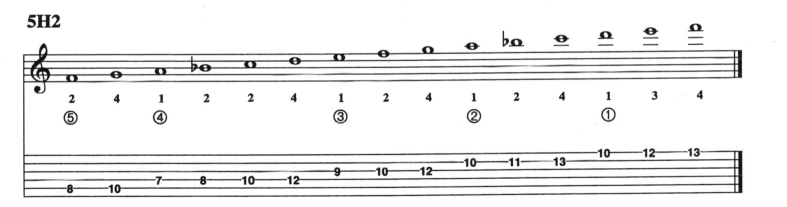

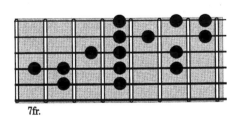

Here's the same thing with the 6H2 and 5H2

Key	Fingering	Starting Fret
C	6H2	8
F	5H2	8
Bb	6H2	6
Eb	5H2	6
Ab	6H2	4
Db	5H2	4
Gb	6H2	2
B	5H2	2
E	5H2	7
A	6H2	5
D	5H2	5
G	6H2	3
C	5H2	3

Solo over II - V - I progressions in all keys.

Example: Dm7 - G7 - CMa7 = use fingering **6H2**

Gm7 - C7 - FMa7 = use fingering **5H2**

Cm7 - F7 - BbMa7 = use fingering **6H2**, etc.

After these six fingerings have been mastered you are ready to connect from one picture to the next.

If the next section of this book does not make any sense, **STOP !!!!** Go back! You need more practice.

The next part should be easy; this is not brain surgery.

Connections

Here's a few examples using fingerings **5V2** and **6V4**.

- If you have practiced the previous fingerings, this is easy.

- I point out these connections because when improvising, you may find the need to access different parts of the fingerboard.

- These examples are not meant to be practiced as a scale fingering but may be used when improvising from the scale.

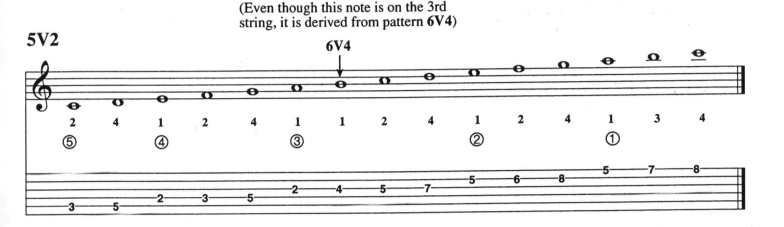

Here's a descending example that uses three fingerings.

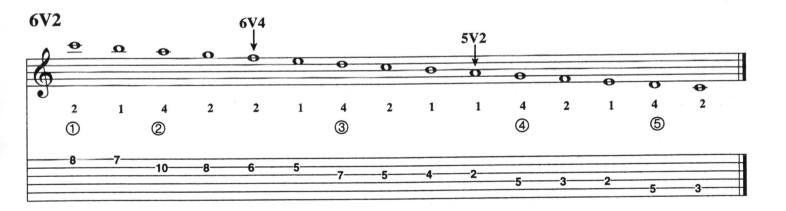

The number of possibilities is endless. The point is to know the six basic fingerings as well as you know how to spell your name. Since the remaining scale fingerings are derived from these six, this type of connection is possible with any scale.

If you want to see these connections in action refer to my hotlicks video *"No Nonsense Jazz Guitar."*

The Dorian Mode

To create the Dorian mode (scale), start a major scale on the second note and keep the fingering the same.

The example below is taken from major scale fingerings **6V2** (C major in this example) but the first note is omitted. This produces a Dorian mode or minor 7th scale.

From 6V2

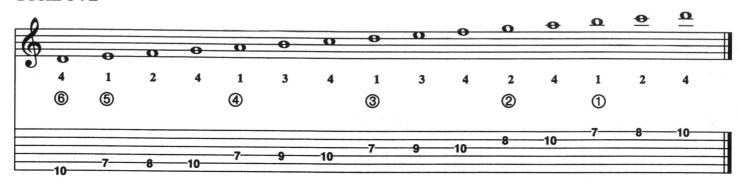

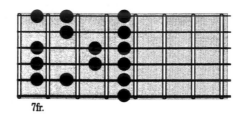

From 5V2

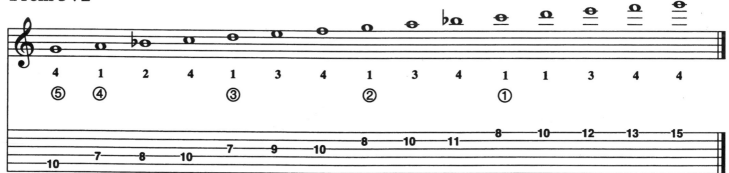

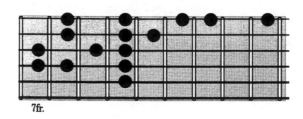

If I take fingering 6V4 and start on the 2nd note I get the following fingering (see example 1).

Example 1

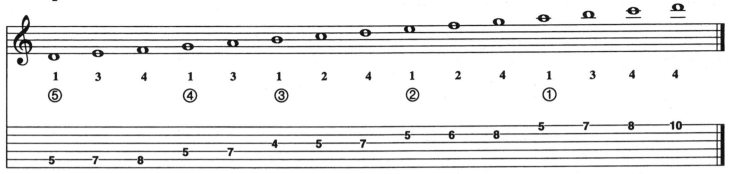

1 3 4 1 3 1 2 4 1 2 4 1 3 4 4

⑤ ④ ③ ② ①

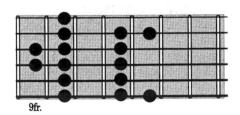

4fr.

In order to keep the pattern of 6th string-5th string intact, take the fingering from example 1 and start it on the 6th string (see example 2). The fingerings are identical except for the last note.

On the next page the pattern is restored starting with fingering example 2.

Example 2

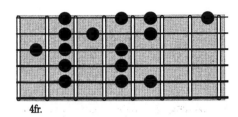

1 3 4 1 3 1 2 4 1 2 4 1 3 4 1

⑥ ⑤ ④ ③ ② ①

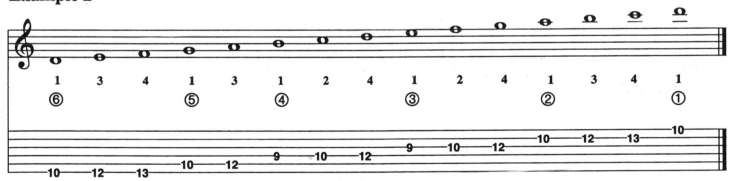

9fr.

From 6V4 but starting on the 6th string

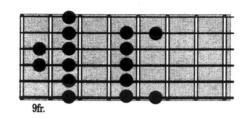

From 5V4

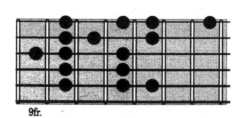

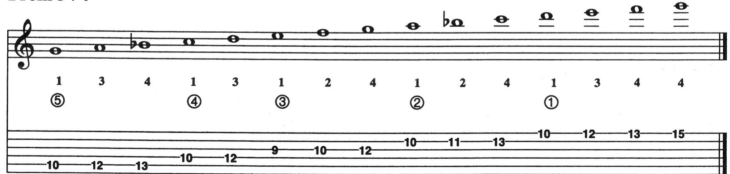

Horizontal Dorian

These are derived from the Horizontal Major Scale fingerings.

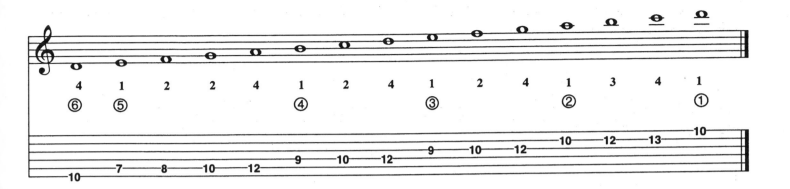

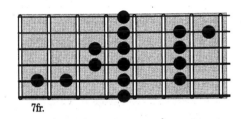

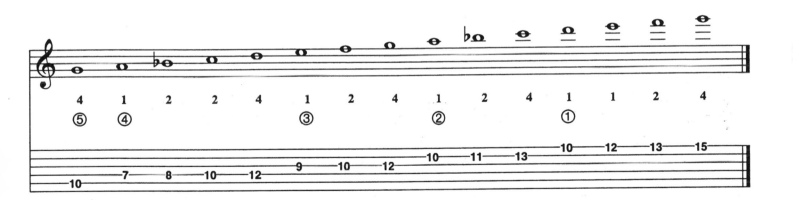

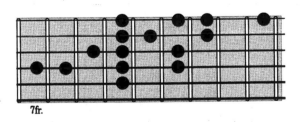

The Mixolydian Mode

The easiest way to create a Mixolydian mode (scale) is to add the three diatonic tones below the root of the parent major scale. In this case I want to create a C Mixolydian. A C Mixolydian is the 5th mode of an F major scale; therefore, I will add the three notes E, D, and C below the F major scale. When I get to the F note I use fingering **5V2** (F Major) and stop on the note C.

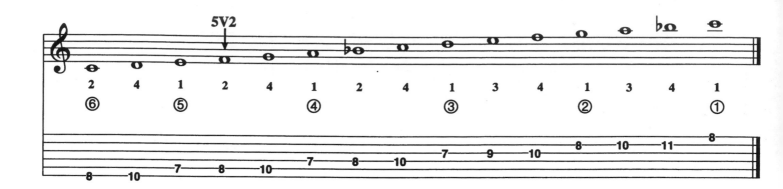

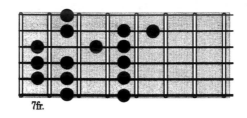

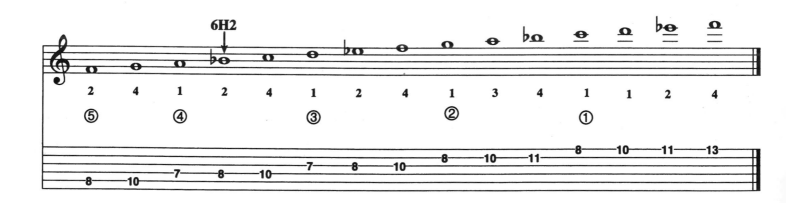

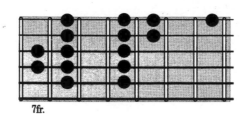

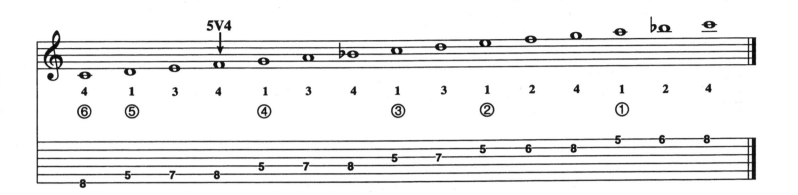

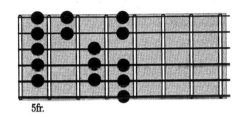

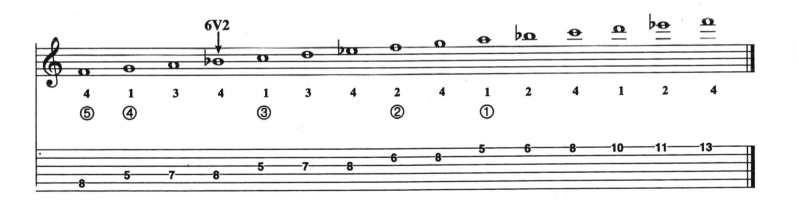

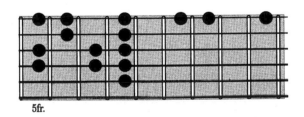

Horizontal Mixolydians

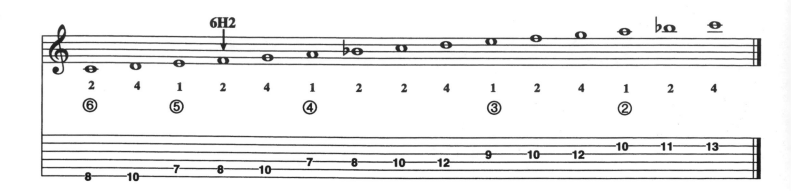

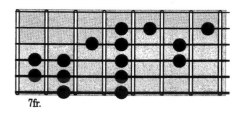

This fingering is derived from the above fingering but starting on the 5th string.

The fingerings are identical.

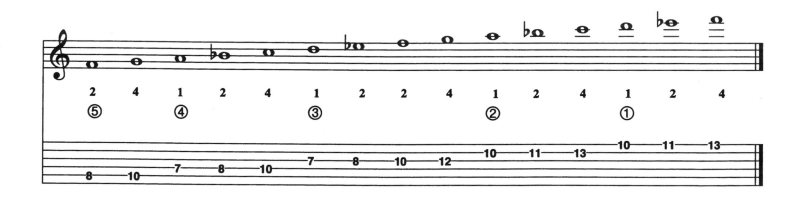

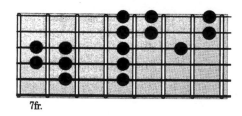

The Natural Minor Scales

To create a natural minor scale, add the two diatonic tones below the root of the relative major scale. In this case I want to create an A natural minor scale. This is the 6th mode of C major; therefore, I will add the two notes B and A below the C major scale. When I get to C, I use fingering **6V4** (C major) and stop on the note A.

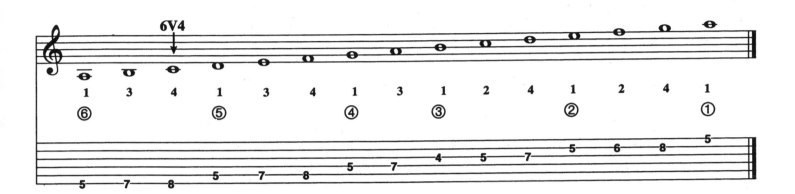

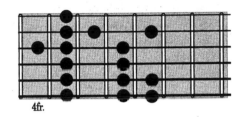

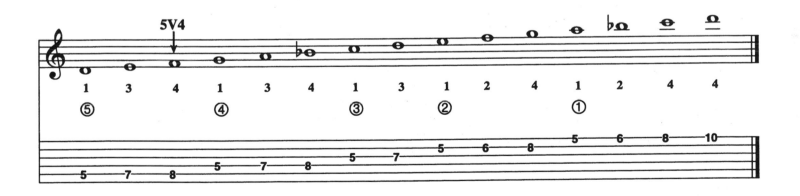

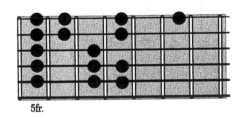

Natural Minors

Horizontal

These fingerings use scale fragments from two different vertical major scale fingerings.

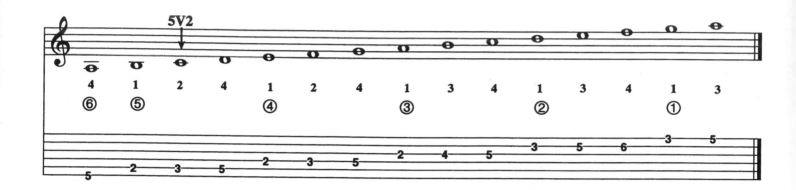

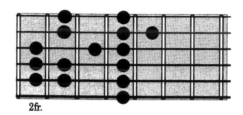

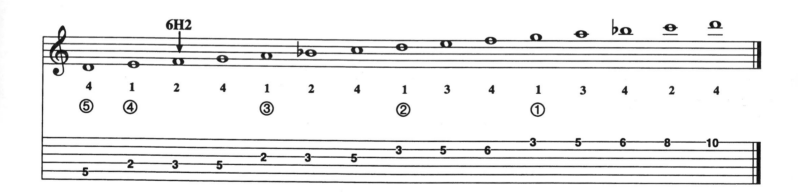

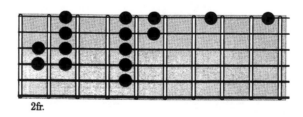

Natural Minors

Horizontal

These fingerings use scale fragments from two different vertical major scale fingerings.

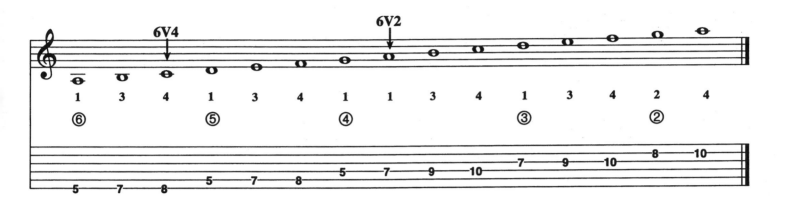

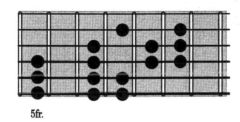

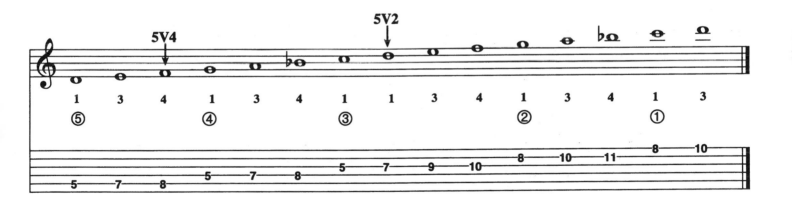

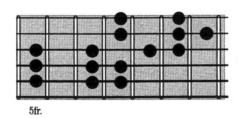

The Harmonic Minor Scales

Raise the 7th tone of the natural minor scale one half step.

Harmonic minors starting with the first finger

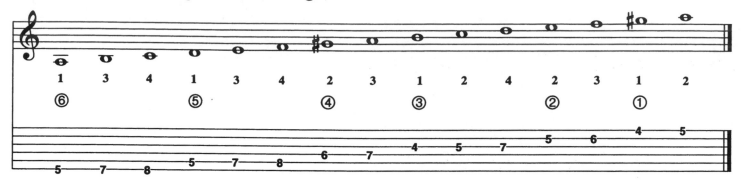

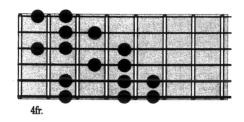

4fr.

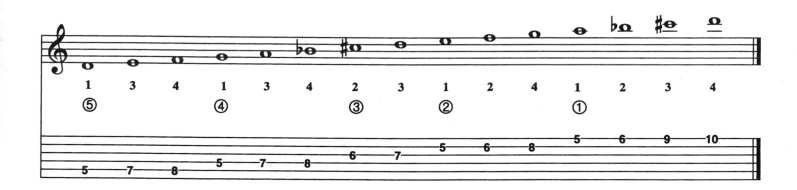

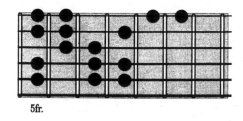

5fr.

Harmonic Minor Scales

Harmonic minors starting with the fourth finger

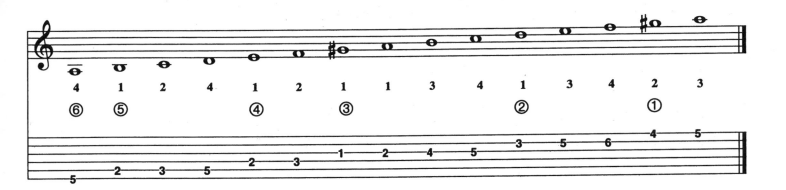

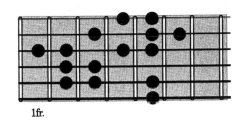

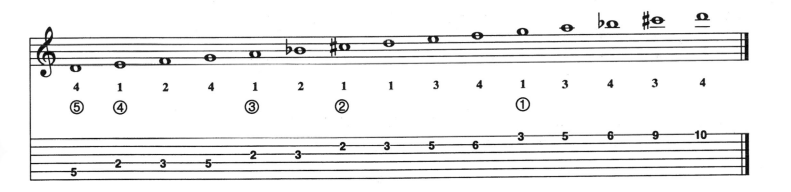

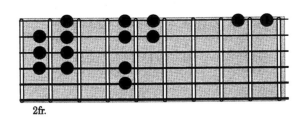

Horizontal Harmonic Minors

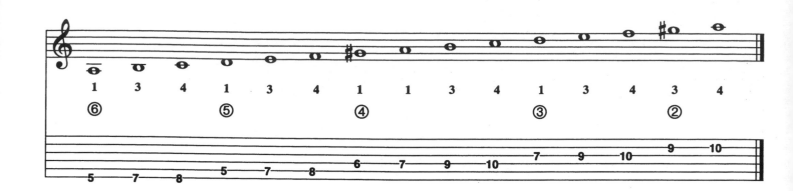

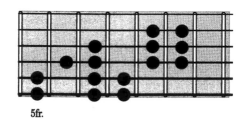

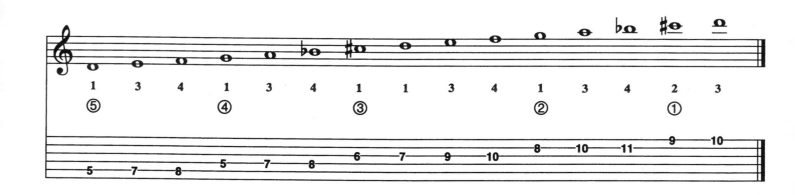

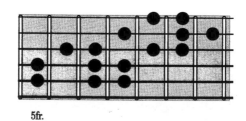

The Melodic Minor Scales

For the melodic minor scale, raise the 7th tone of the Dorian mode one half step.

For me this is easier than making the adjustment from the natural or the harmonic minor.

Melodic minors starting with the first finger

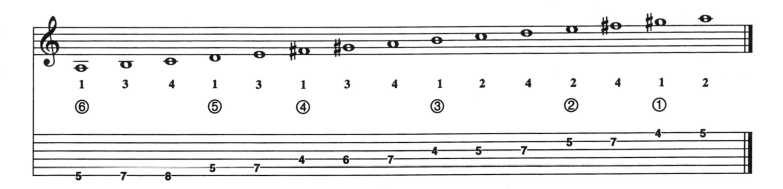

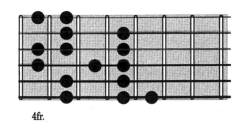

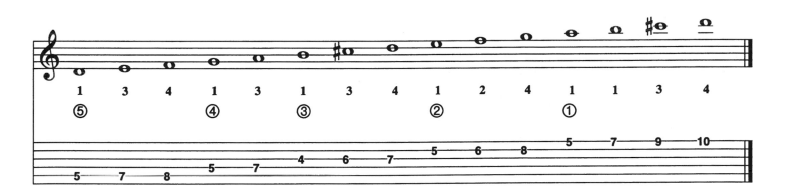

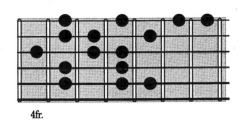

Melodic Minors

Melodic minors starting with the fourth finger

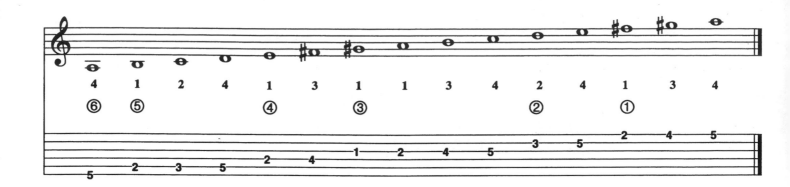

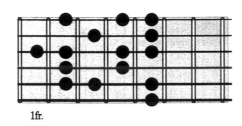

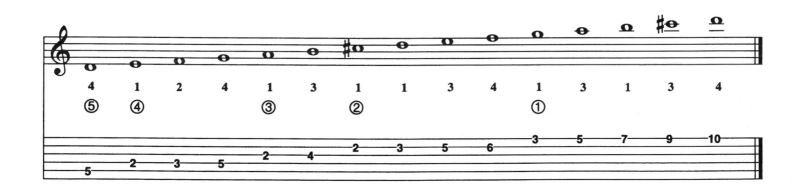

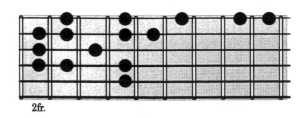

Melodic Minors Horizontal

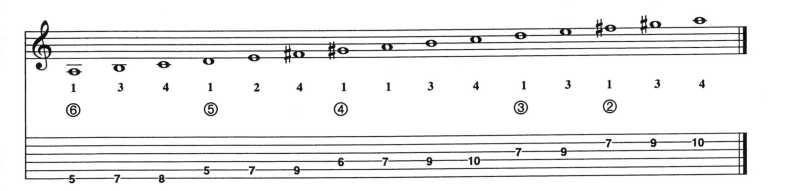

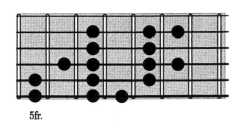

5fr.

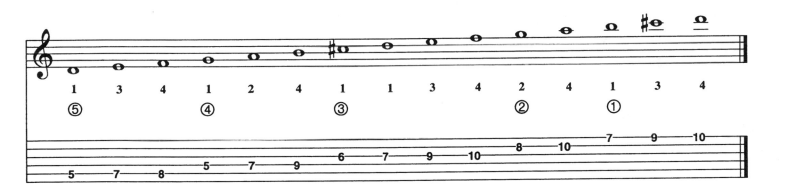

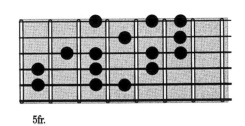

5fr.

Conclusion

I hope this small reference text helps to improve your understanding of the fingerboard. Unfortunately, space did not permit the inclusion of some of the altered scales. However, all the modes of the harmonic and melodic minor scales are easily derived.

For example, the diminished whole-tone scale is the 7th mode of the melodic minor. For a major pentatonic scale remove the 2nd and 4th degree of any major scale. The use of such scales is somewhat involved and would probably require a separate book. If you have questions email me at jimmy@jimmybruno.com.

A very special thanks to the following medical doctors who have helped me regain my health:

Dr. Leonard Harmon

Dr. Mitchel A. Smith

Dr. Dave Rudnick

Dr. Howard Klein

Dr. Eric Goosenberg

Dr. Samaha

Dr. Barry Kayes

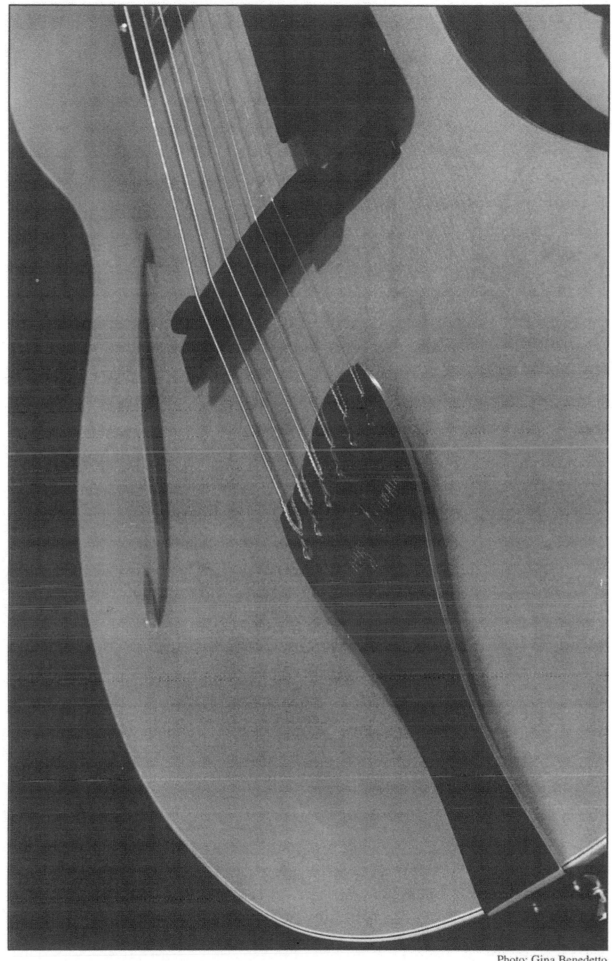

Photo: Gina Benedetto

Body/tailpiece view of BENEDETTO "Jimmy Bruno" Model prototype
(Note: Jimmy's name engraved in tailpiece)

BENEDETTO "Jimmy Bruno" Model prototype

Headstock of BENEDETTO "Jimmy Bruno" Model prototype

BENEDETTO "Jimmy Bruno" Model prototype with Cool Cat, Luna.